JUMPIN' JIM'S
UKULELE
FAVORITES

T0059095

Edited by Jim Beloff

Cover Design by Elizabeth Maihock Beloff
Copy Editing Ronny S. Schiff

© 1993 FLEA MARKET MUSIC, INCORPORATED
Visit us at www.fleamarketmusic.com

Exclusively Distributed by

HAL•LEONARD®
CORPORATION
7777 W. BLUEMOUND RD. P.O. BOX 13819 MILWAUKEE, WI 53213

FOREWORD

S ometime around the beginning of 1992, at the Pasadena Rose Bowl flea market, I happened upon an old tenor Martin ukulele. The end result of that chance purchase is what you are holding in your hands. In very short order, I became totally smitten with the instrument and, especially, a wealth of out-of-print uke songbooks, often featuring remarkably sophisticated arrangements of great classic songs.

Three books in particular, featuring arrangements by Ukulele Ike (see page 6), were my greatest inspiration. As time wore on, I discovered more and more great uke folios and became convinced that many of the jewel-like arrangements in these books deserved to see the light of day once more. This, despite the fact that the ukulele was not quite the "instrument du jour" that it had been in the 'twenties, 'fifties and, for a brief moment, during the Tiny Tim era.

Unfazed, I pursued the reprinting of some of my favorite arrangements. Part of my belief in this project stemmed from the fact that every time I took my uke out at a family gathering, people of all ages would gather around to sing and/or learn these great songs.

So, to you, kind purchaser, I wish as many pleasant hours practicing and performing these tunes and arrangements as I have had.

My gratitude goes to the many who helped make this book a reality. In particular, Ronny Schiff, Helene Blue, Mary Vandenberg, Dave Olsen, Shep Stern, Don Maihock, Marvin Beloff, Jay Morgenstern, Gene Sculatti, Fred Sokolow, Ian Whitcomb and especially my wife, Liz, who says the reason I like the uke so much is because I can play it lying down.

—Jumpin' Jim

HOW TO USE THIS BOOK

The beauty of the arrangements in this book is that, in many cases, by playing through the diagrammed chords you can actually hear the melody (e.g., "Don't Blame Me," "We're Off To See The Wizard," "More Than You Know"). This method of arranging, known as chord soloing, is what can make the experience of playing the uke so challenging and satisfying.

Because each song is presented with chord diagrams, it is not essential to be able to read music to enjoy this book. There are, however, a few points to be made about the various tunings that are used here. While most uke experts today recommend that all soprano, concert and tenor ukes be tuned GCEA (C major 6th tuning), this has not always been the case. In fact, in the 'fifties the universal tuning was ADF♯B (D major 6th tuning). Other tunings include the FB♭DG (B♭ major 6th tuning), and the one I prefer to tune my tenor to: DGBE (G major 6th tuning), which is the same as the tuning of the baritone uke or the bottom four strings of the guitar. In all cases, I like these "My Dog Has Fleas" tunings with the lowered third string.

The chord chart on the following two pages is for ukes tuned GCEA: **C major 6th**

G C E A

In the ADF♯B tuning, positions and fingerings remain the same, but the chord names change one whole step up...

For example: **All C chords become D**

In the DGBE tuning (baritone uke) chord names change down a fourth...

For example: **All C chords become G**

Alternate Tunings...

D major 6th **B♭ major 6th** **G major 6th**

A D F♯ B   F B♭ D G   D G B E

4

CHORD CHART FOR UKULELE

Tune Ukulele
G C E A

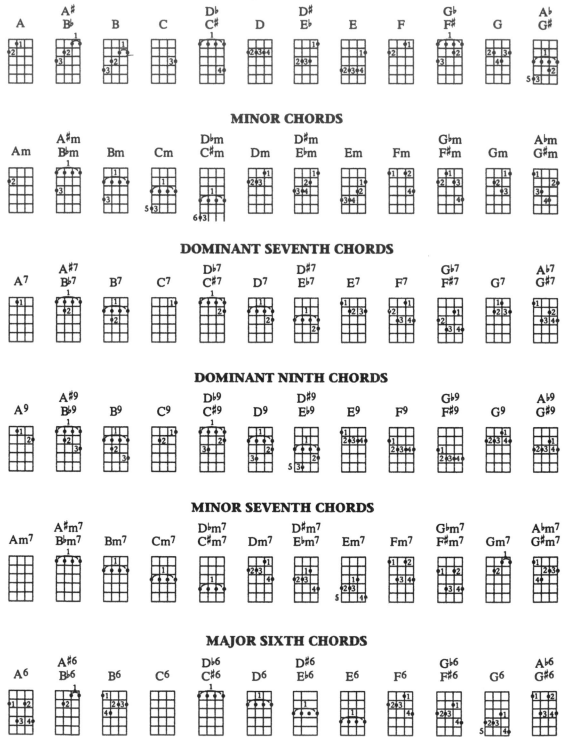

MINOR SIXTH CHORDS

MAJOR SEVENTH CHORDS

DOMINANT SEVENTH CHORDS WITH RAISED FIFTH (7th+5)

DOMINANT SEVENTH CHORDS WITH LOWERED FIFTH (7th-5)

AUGMENTED FIFTH CHORDS (AUG. or +)

DIMINISHED SEVENTH CHORDS (Dim.)

UKULELE IKE

Many of the arrangements in this book were created by Cliff Edwards, also known as Ukulele Ike. Born June 14th, 1895 in Hannibal, Missouri, he started playing in St. Louis saloons, sometimes playing ukulele and kazoo when the bar didn't have a piano. After traveling around, working in carnivals and odd jobs, he teamed with stuttering comedian/pianist Joe Frisco, initially working vaudeville and then moving up to big engagements in Chicago. It was there that a barman, who couldn't remember Edwards' name, tagged him "Ike" and the "Ukulele" just seemed to go right along with it. Then he headed off to Broadway where he performed in *Lady Be Good* ('24) (in which he introduced "Fascinating Rhythm") and other musicals and revues.

The first known recording of Edwards was playing kazoo on "Virginia Blues," issued on Fountain Records in 1922. Even though he was playing in various Broadway shows, his subsequent recordings displayed definite jazz chops, often in the company of the day's finest jazz musicians.

A favorite in movies during the transition from silents to talkies – especially in light comedy and musical roles, he introduced "Singin' In The Rain" in the *Hollywood Revue of '29*. During the 'thirties and 'forties, he appeared in 47 movies, including *Gone With Wind*. In 1939, Walt Disney chose him to be the voice of Jiminy Cricket in *Pinocchio*, where he sang the classic "When You Wish Upon A Star."

In the early 'fifties, he was once more employed by Disney to bring back the Jiminy Cricket character and others to television and on several children's recordings.

Cliff Edwards' legacy was two-fold: As a great ukulele player he was responsible for popularizing the ukulele in the 'twenties – a time when they began adding ukulele chord frames to sheet music. As a singer, it has been suggested that he inspired great singers such as Fred Astaire and Bing Crosby. His three collections of ukulele arrangements, published by Big 3 Music, were amongst the biggest-selling collections of ukulele music ever.

Edwards died July 17, 1971, in Hollywood, California.

SONGS IN THIS COLLECTION
ARRANGED BY UKULELE IKE
• I'm Always Chasing Rainbows • Ramona
• More Than You Know • Mairzy Doats
• Over The Rainbow • Don't Blame Me
• We're Off To See The Wizard
• The Aba Daba Honeymoon • Whispering
• The Whiffenpoof Song • The Boy Next Door
• Five Foot Two, Eyes Of Blue • Once In A While

Photo courtesy of Ian Whitcomb/ITW Industries © 1992

By The Light Of The Silvery Moon

Words by
ED MADDEN

Music by
GUS EDWARDS

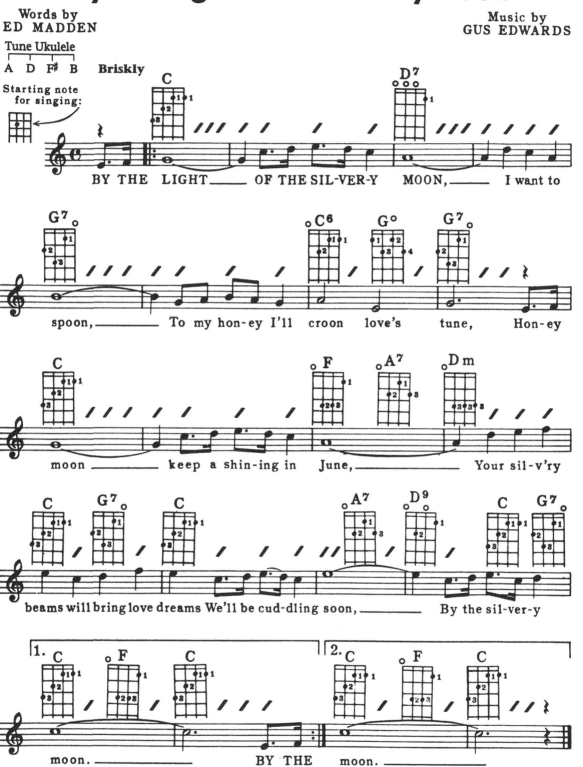

The Aba Daba Honeymoon

By
ARTHUR FIELDS *and*
WALTER DONOVAN

way. "Ab-a, dab-a, dab-a, dab-a, dab-a, dab-a, dab," means

"Monk, I   love but   you,"   "Bab-a, dab-a, dab," in

mon-key-talk,means"Chimp, I   love you   too."   Then the

big   ba-boon,one   night   in   June, He   mar-ried   them,and

ver-y   soon They   went   up-on— their   ab-a, dab-a   hon-ey-

moon. _____   moon. _____

The Birth Of The Blues

Words by
B. G. DE SYLVA
and **LEW BROWN**
A.S.C.A.P.

Music by
RAY HENDERSON
A.S.C.A.P.

They heard the breeze in the trees Sing-ing weird mel-o-dies And they made that ____ The start of the blues. ____ And from a jail came the wail Of a down heart-ed frail, And they played that ____ As part of the

The Boy Next Door

Words and Music by
HUGH MARTIN
and **RALPH BLANE**

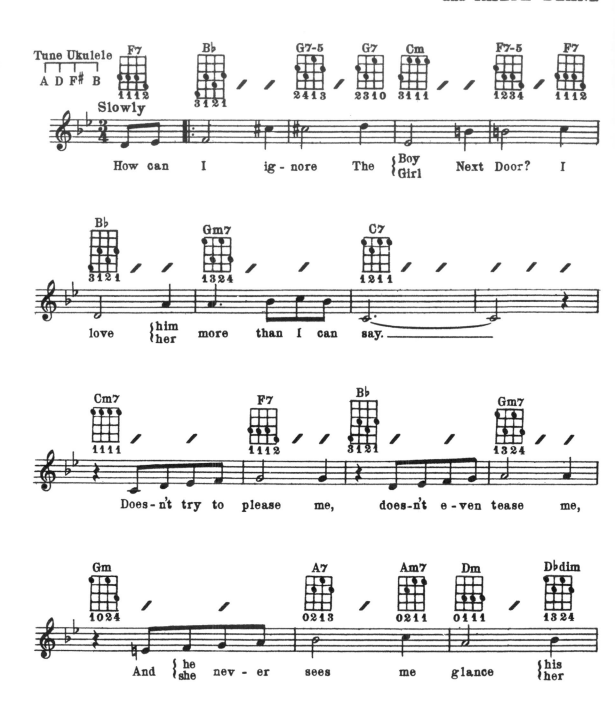

Bye Bye Blackbird

Lyric by
MORT DIXON

Music by
RAY HENDERSON

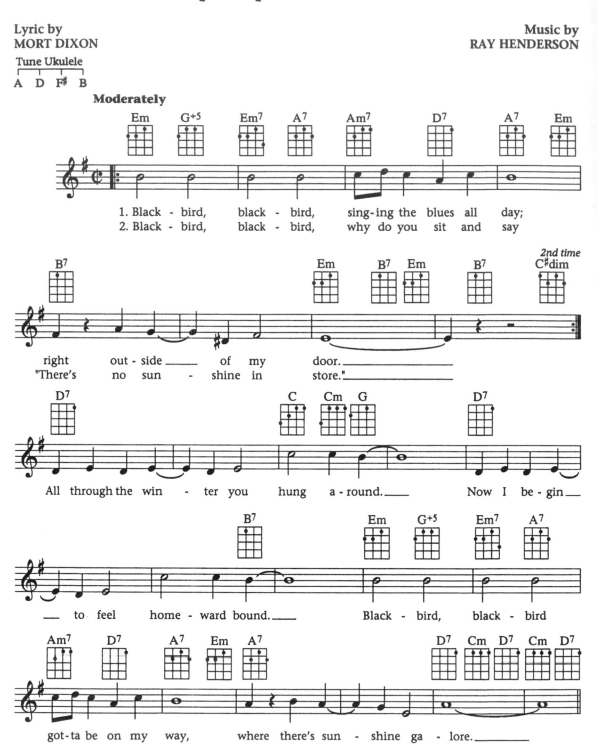

Dancing In The Dark

Words by
HOWARD DIETZ

Music by
ARTHUR SCHWARTZ

Look - ing for the light_____ Of a new love to bright - en up the night,_____ I have you, love, And we can face the mu - sic to - geth - - er,

1. Danc - ing in the dark._____

2. Danc - ing in the dark._____

Deep Purple

Words by
MITCHELL PARISH

Music by
PETER DE ROSE

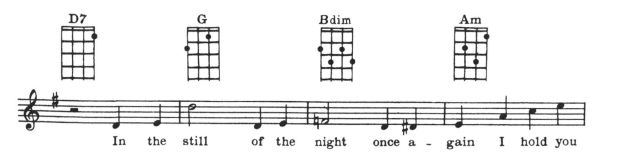

In the still of the night once a - gain I hold you

tight, Tho' you're gone, your love lives on when moon-light beams, _____

— And as long as my heart will beat, Lov - er, we'll

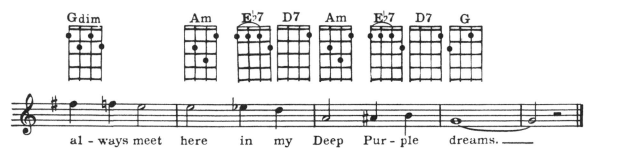

al - ways meet here in my Deep Pur - ple dreams. _____

Don't Blame Me

Lyric by
DOROTHY FIELDS

Melody by
JIMMY McHUGH

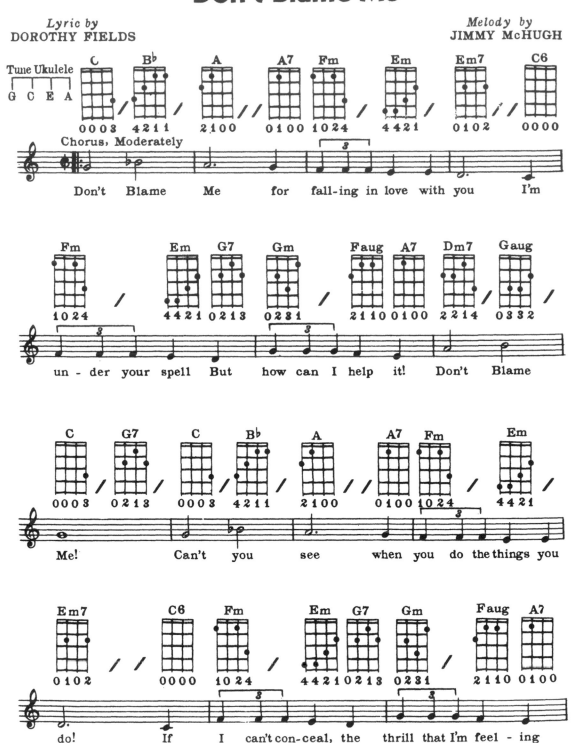

Don't Get Unused To Me

Words and Music by
JIM BELOFF

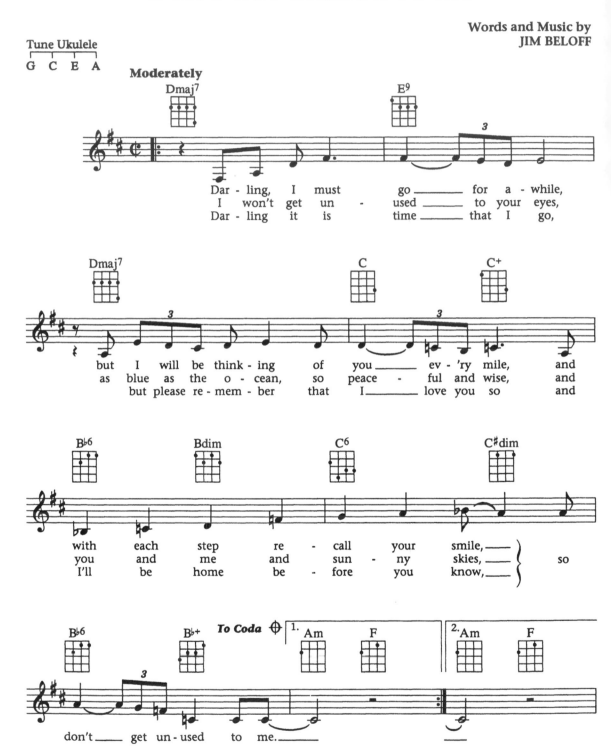

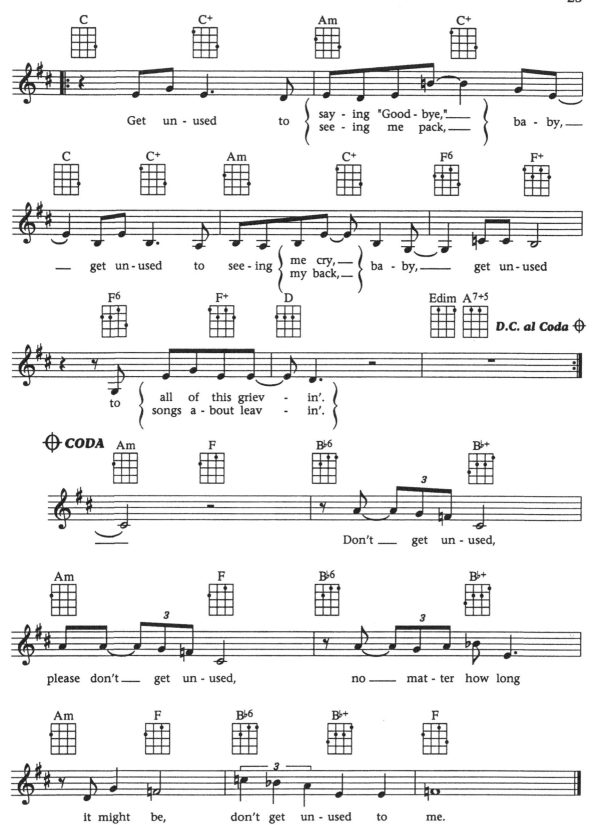

Dream A Little Dream Of Me

Words by GUS KAHN

Music by WILBUR SCHWANDT
and FABIAN ANDREE

Tune Ukulele

G C E A

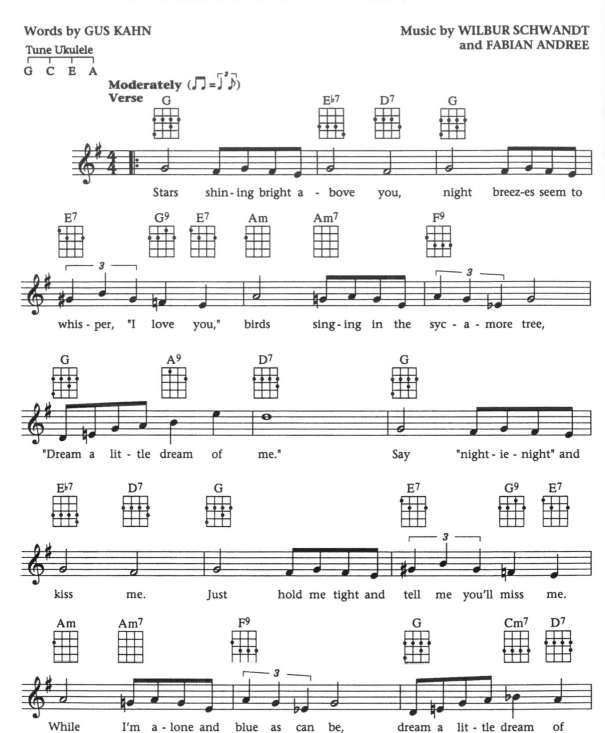

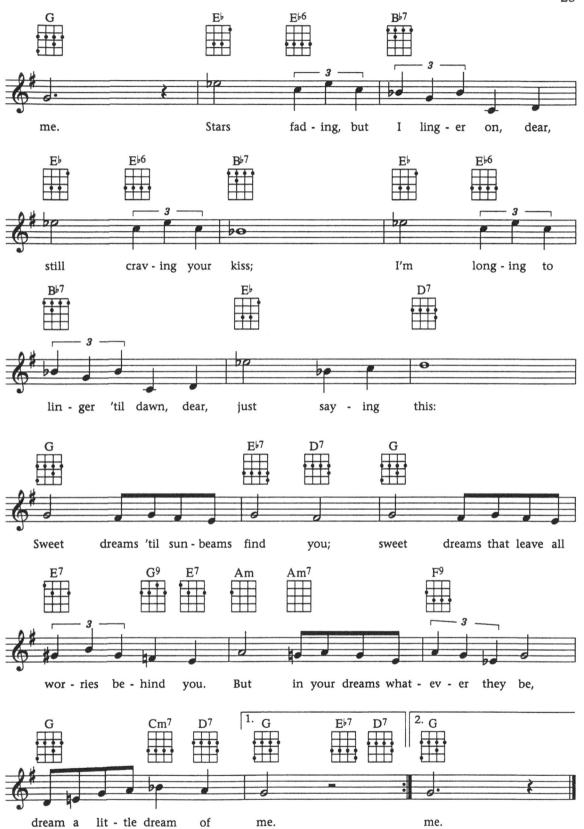

Five Foot Two, Eyes Of Blue
(Has Anybody Seen My Girl?)

Lyrics by
SAM LEWIS and
JOE YOUNG

Music by
RAY HENDERSON

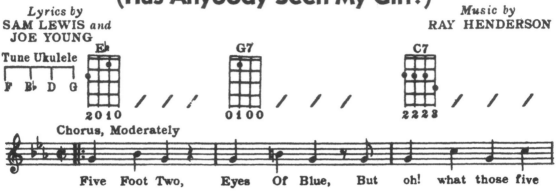

Five Foot Two, Eyes Of Blue, But oh! what those five

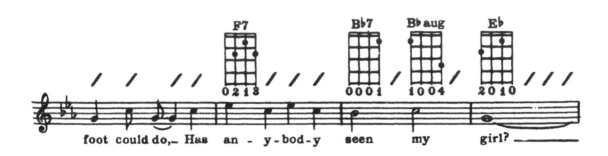

foot could do,— Has an - y-bod-y seen my girl?——

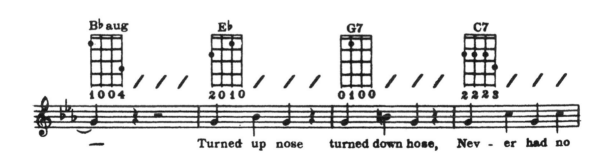

Turned up nose turned down hose, Nev - er had no

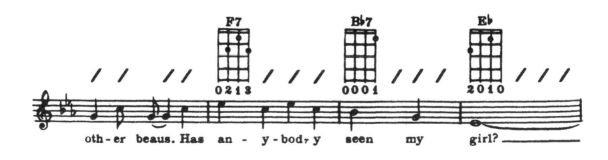

oth - er beaus. Has an - y-bod-y seen my girl?——

Good Night Sweetheart

American Version by
RUDY VALLEE

by
RAY NOBLE
JIMMY CAMPBELL
REG CONNELLY

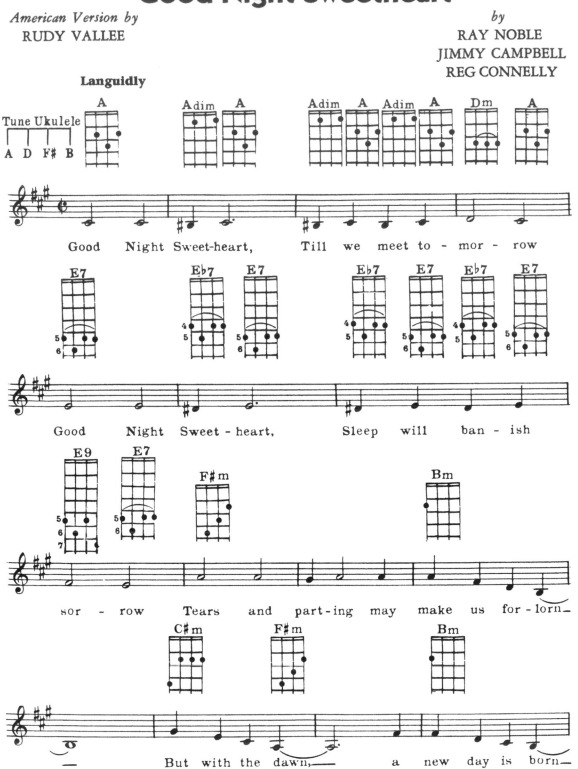

Good Night Sweet-heart, Till we meet to-mor-row

Good Night Sweet-heart, Sleep will ban-ish

sor-row Tears and part-ing may make us for-lorn

But with the dawn, a new day is born

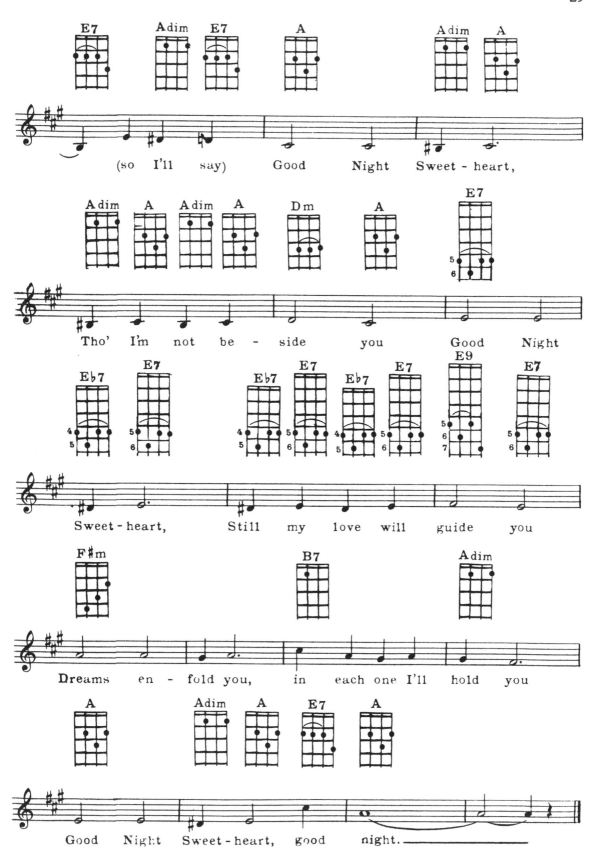

(so I'll say) Good Night Sweet - heart,

Tho' I'm not be - side you Good Night

Sweet - heart, Still my love will guide you

Dreams en - fold you, in each one I'll hold you

Good Night Sweet - heart, good night._____

Hi-Lili, Hi-Lo

Words by
HELEN DEUTSCH

Music by
BRONISLAU KAPER

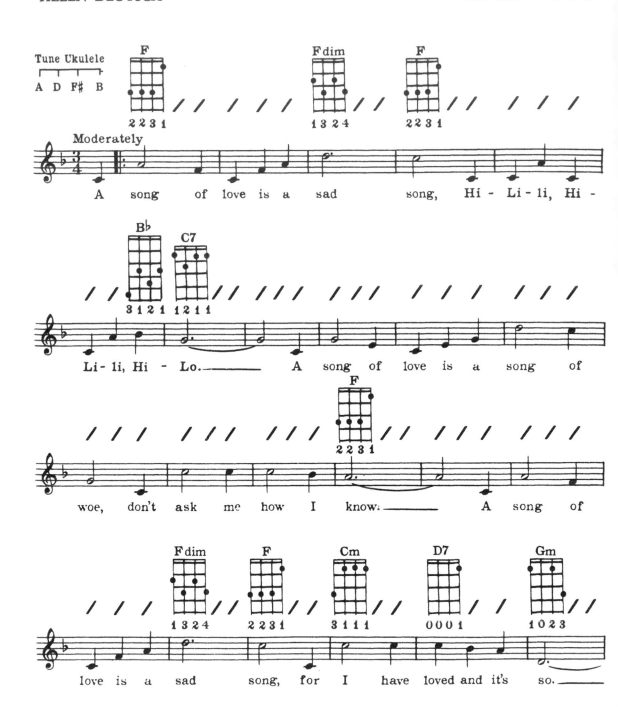

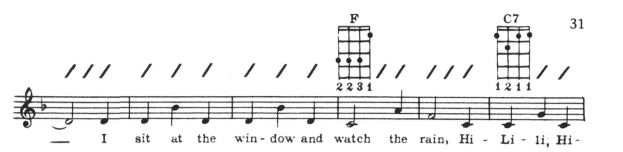

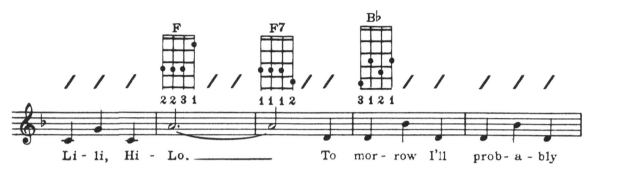

I sit at the win-dow and watch the rain, Hi - Li - li, Hi-

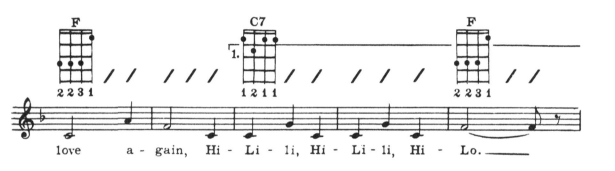

Li - li, Hi - Lo. _____ To mor - row I'll prob- a - bly

love a - gain, Hi - Li - li, Hi - Li - li, Hi - Lo. _____

A Li - li, Hi - Li - li, Hi - Lo. _____

I Don't Want To Set The World On Fire

Words by EDDIE SEILER
and SOL MARCUS

Music by BENNIE BENJAMIN
and EDDIE DURHAM

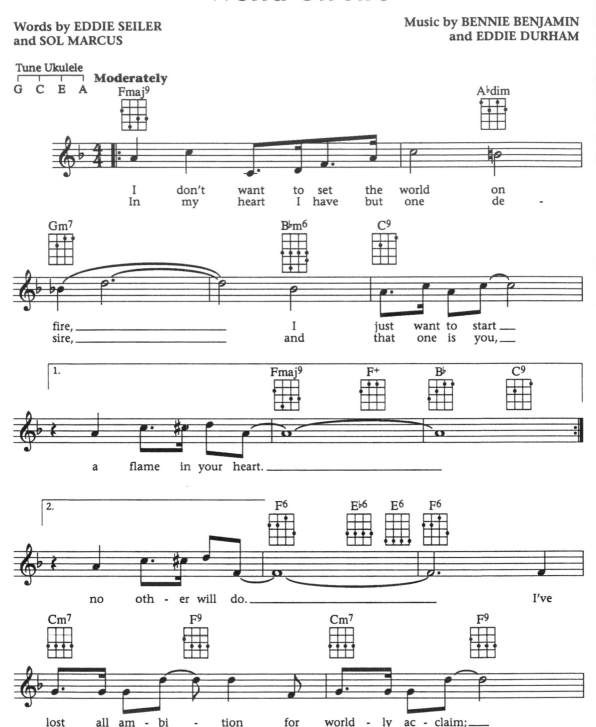

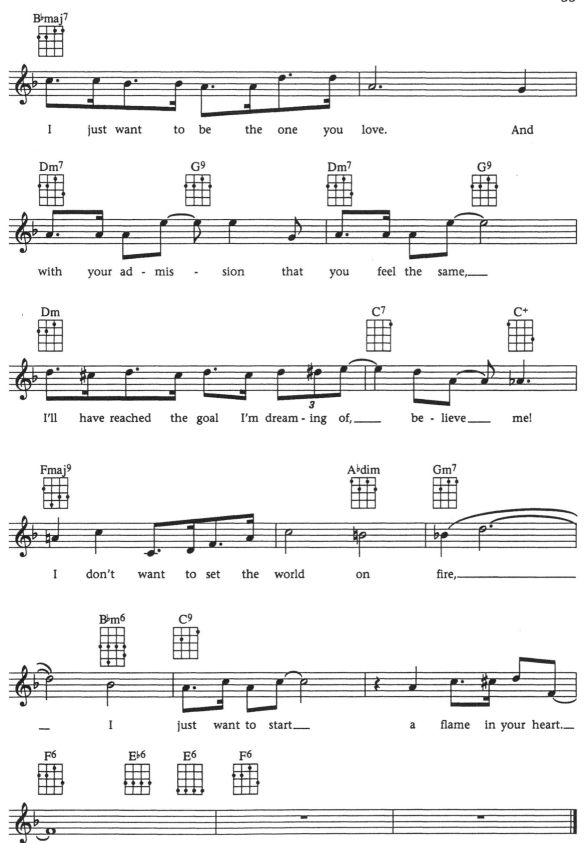

If They Can Put A Man On The Moon

Words and Music by
JIM BELOFF

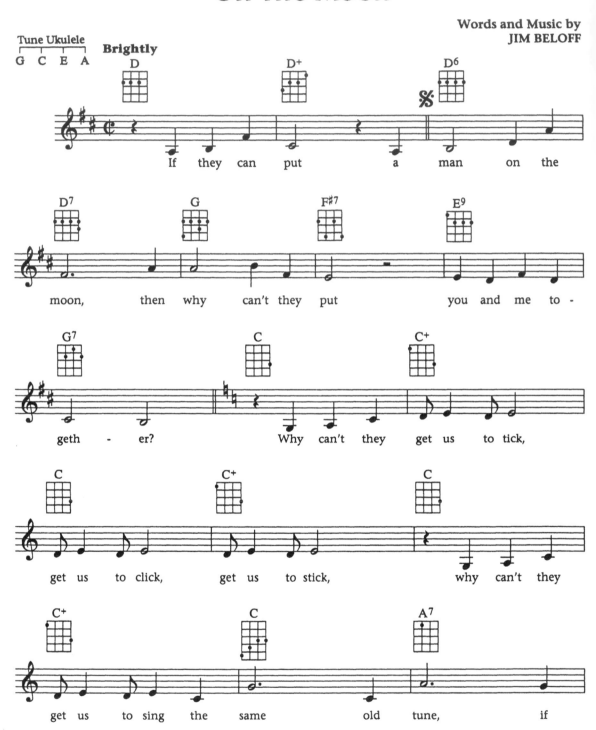

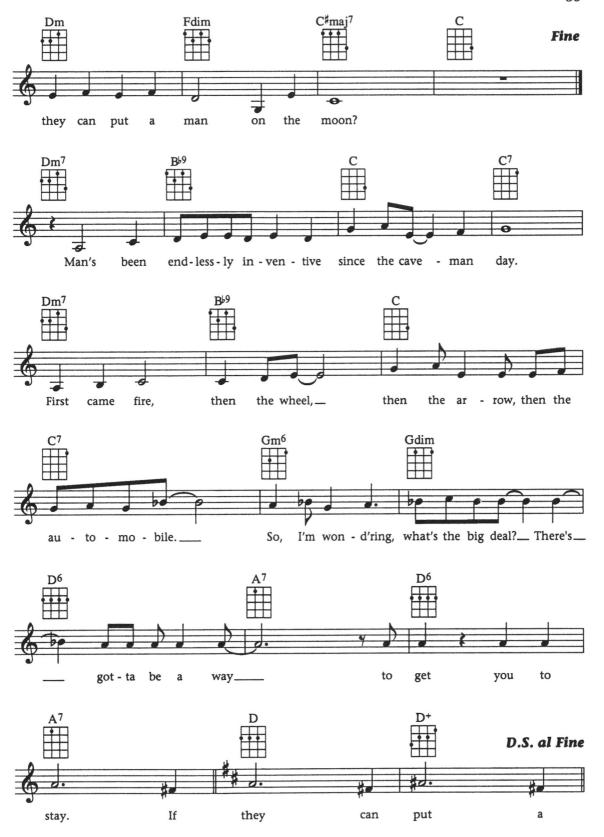

they can put a man on the moon?

Man's been end-less-ly in-ven-tive since the cave-man day.

First came fire, then the wheel,— then the ar-row, then the

au-to-mo-bile.— So, I'm won-d'ring, what's the big deal?— There's—

— got-ta be a way— to get you to

stay. If they can put a

I Got It Bad
(And That Ain't Good)

Words by
PAUL WEBSTER

Music by
DUKE ELLINGTON

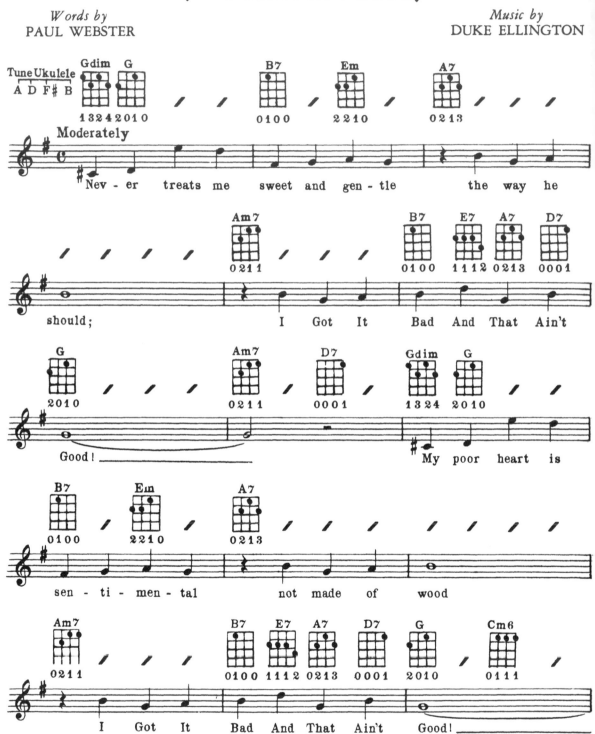

I'm Always Chasing Rainbows

Lyric by
JOSEPH McCARTHY

Music by
HARRY CARROLL

I'm In The Mood For Love

Lyric and Melody by
JIMMY McHUGH *and*
DOROTHY FIELDS

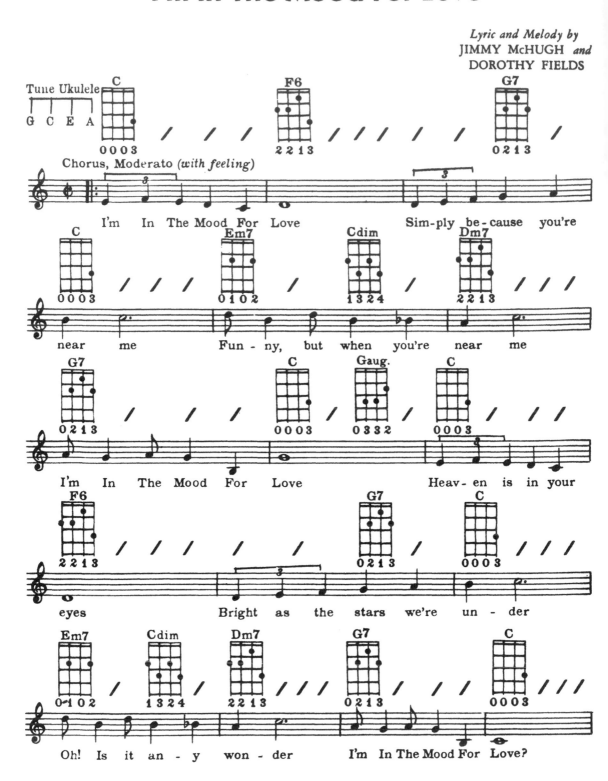

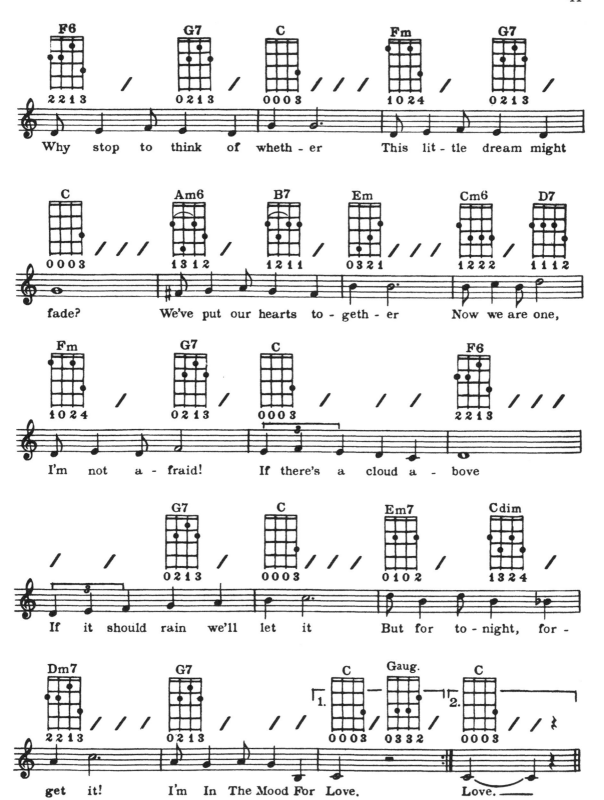

Mairzy Doats

Words and Music by
MILTON DRAKE
AL HOFFMAN
JERRY LIVINGSTON

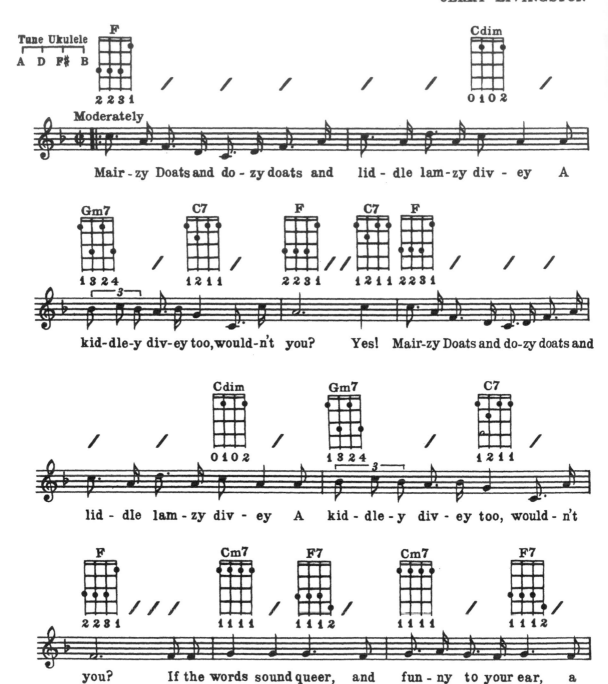

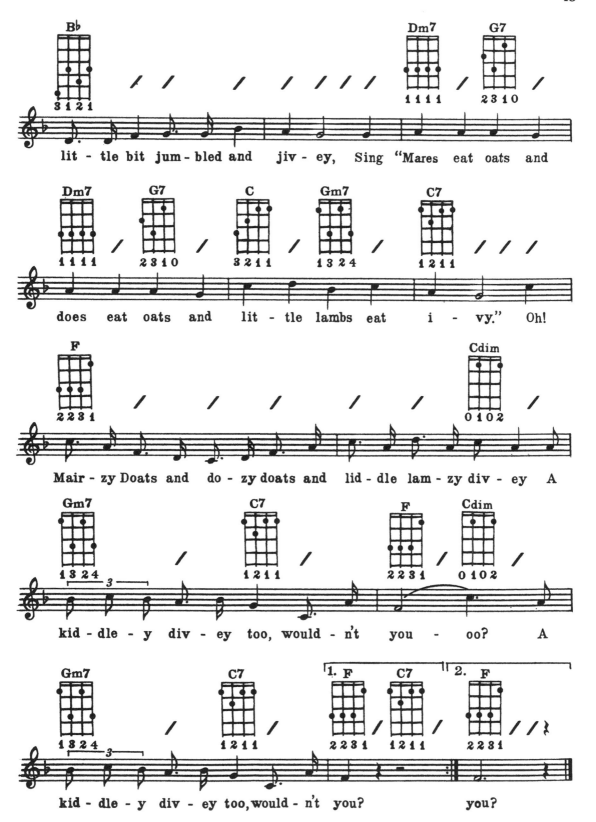

lit - tle bit jum - bled and jiv - ey, Sing "Mares eat oats and

does eat oats and lit - tle lambs eat i - vy." Oh!

Mair - zy Doats and do - zy doats and lid - dle lam - zy div - ey A

kid - dle - y div - ey too, would - n't you - oo? A

kid - dle - y div - ey too, would - n't you? you?

More Than You Know

Lyrics by
WILLIAM ROSE and
EDWARD ELISCU

Music by
VINCENT YOUMANS

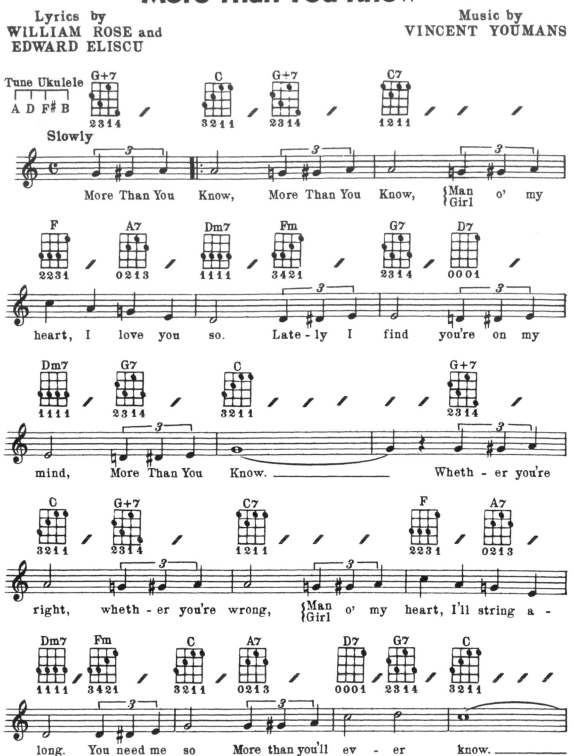

Once In A While

Words by
BUD GREEN

Music by
MICHAEL EDWARDS

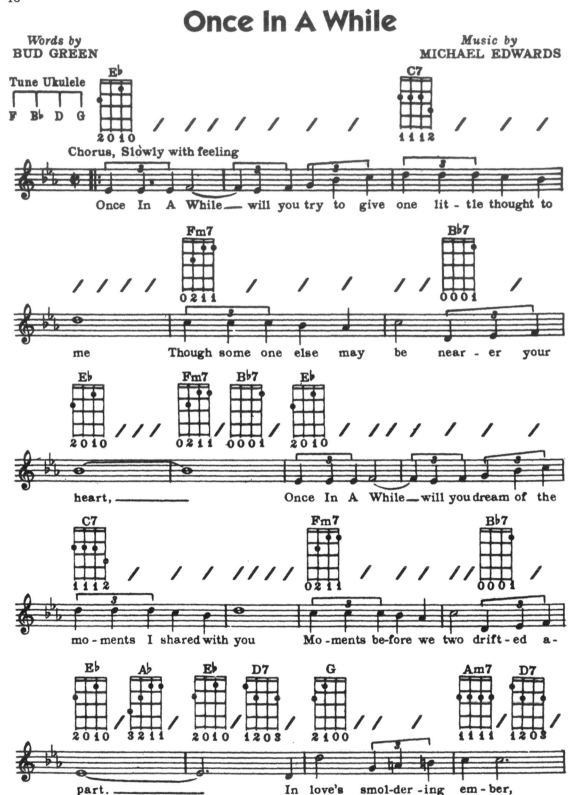

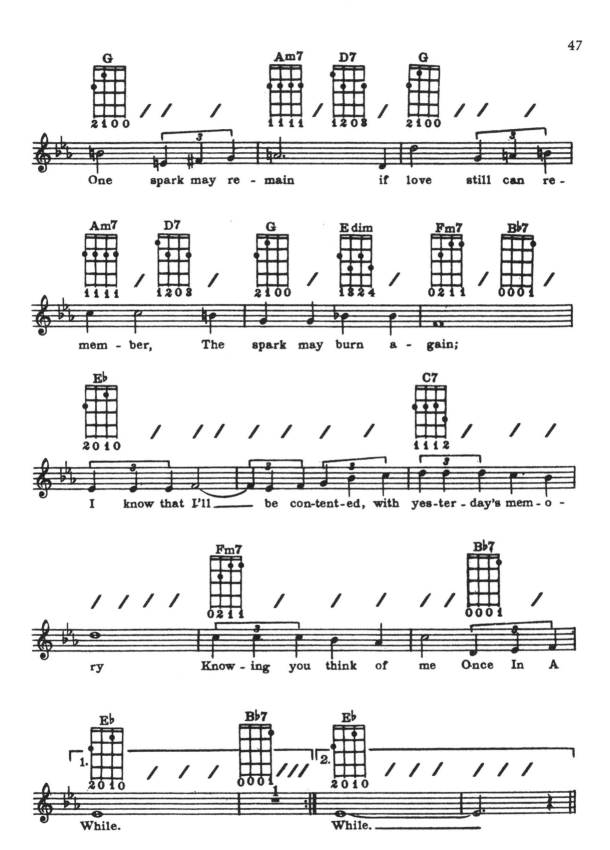

Over The Rainbow

Lyric by
E.Y. HARBURG

Music by
HAROLD ARLEN

true.   Some-day I'll wish up-on a star and wake up where the clouds are far be-

hind   me. _____   Where troub-les melt like lem-on drops, a-

way a-bove the chim-ney tops that's where you'll find   me.   Some - where

O - ver The Rain-bow blue - birds   fly,   Birds   fly

O - ver The Rain-bow, why then, oh   why can't I?   I?

Ramona

Lyric by
L. WOLFE GILBERT

Music by
MABEL WAYNE

Ra - mon - a, I hear the mis-sion bells a - bove, ___ Ra - mon - a, they're ring-ing out our song of love, ___ I press you, ca - ress you, and bless the day you taught me to care, To al - ways re-mem - ber the ram - bling rose you wear in your hair, Ra-

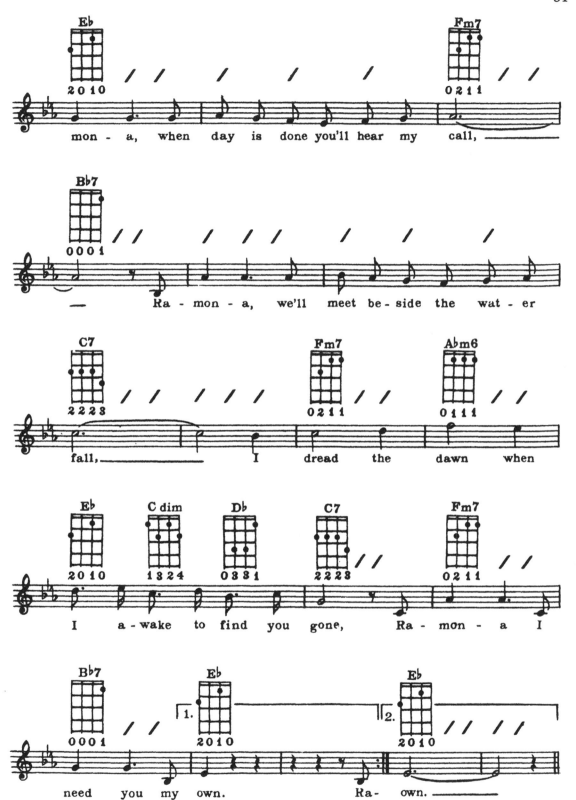

That Lucky Old Sun
(Just Rolls Around Heaven All Day)

Lyric by
HAVEN GILLESPIE

Music by
BEASLEY SMITH

Chorus, Moderately

Up in the morn-in' out on the job, work like the dev-il for my pay, But That Luck-y Old Sun has noth-in' to do but roll a-round heav-en all day. Fuss with my wo-man, toil for my kids Sweat 'til I'm wrin-kled and gray, While That Luck-y Old Sun has noth-in' to do but roll a-round heav-en all

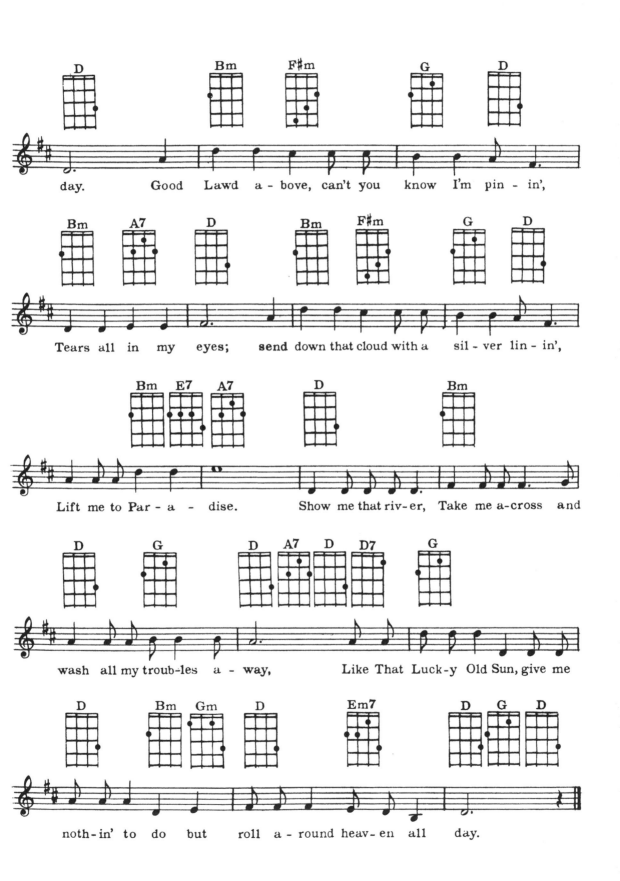

Tip-Toe Thru' The Tulips With Me

Lyric by
AL DUBIN

Music by
JOE BURKE

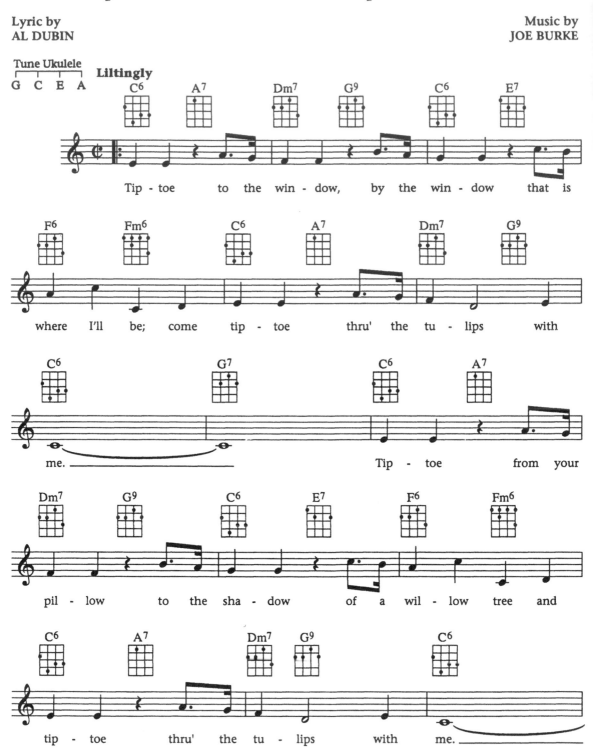

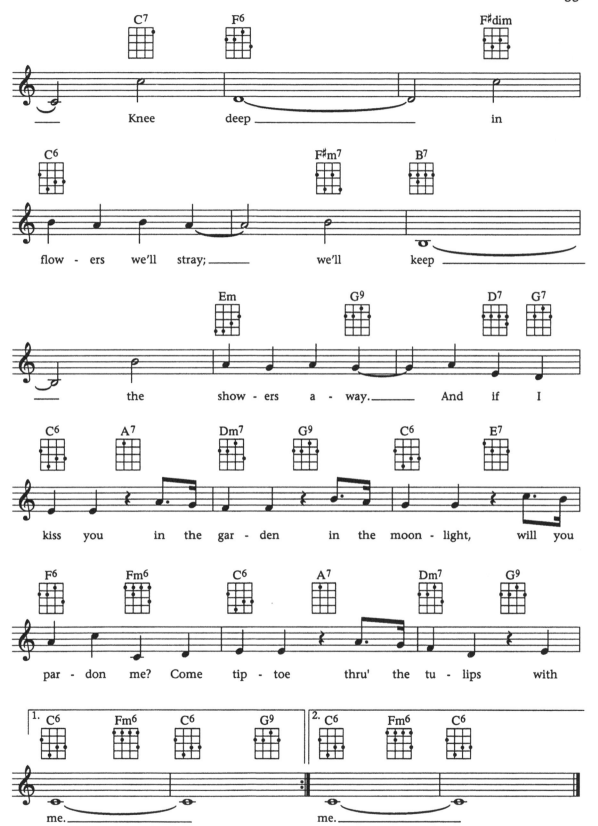

The Ukulele Song

Words and Music by
SHEPARD STERN

We're Off To See The Wizard
(That Wonderful Wizard Of Oz)

Lyric by
E.Y. HARBURG

Music by
HAROLD ARLEN

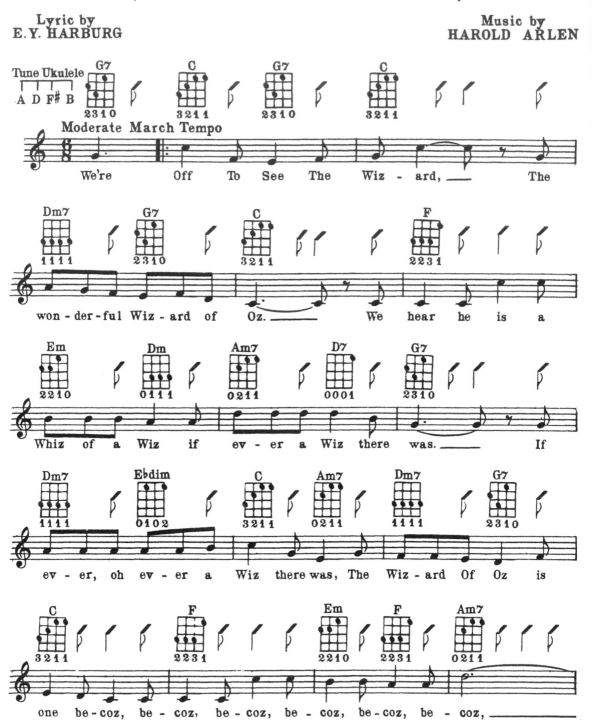

Be - coz of the won - der - ful

things he does. *(Whistle)* _____ We're

Off To See The Wiz - ard, ___ The won - der - ful Wiz - ard of

Oz. _____

We're

The Whiffenpoof Song
(Baa! Baa! Baa!)

Revision by
RUDY VALLEE

by
MEADE MINNIGERODE
GEORGE S. POMEROY
TOD B. GALLOWAY

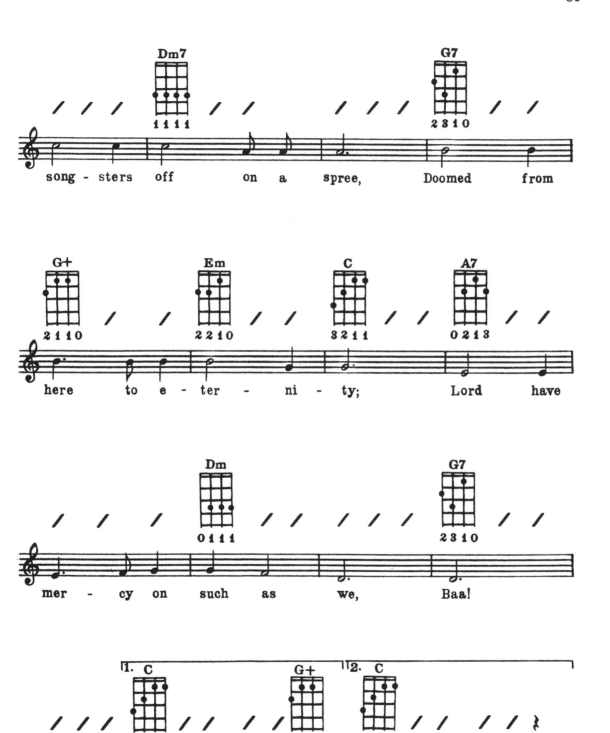

Whispering

Words and Music by
JOHN SCHONBERGER
RICHARD COBURN
VINCENT ROSE

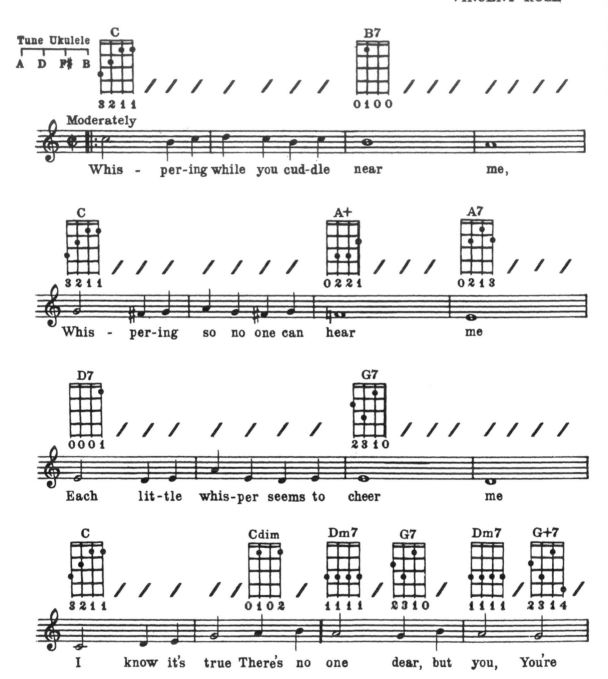

Whis - per-ing while you cud-dle near me,

Whis - per-ing so no one can hear me

Each lit-tle whis-per seems to cheer me

I know it's true There's no one dear, but you, You're

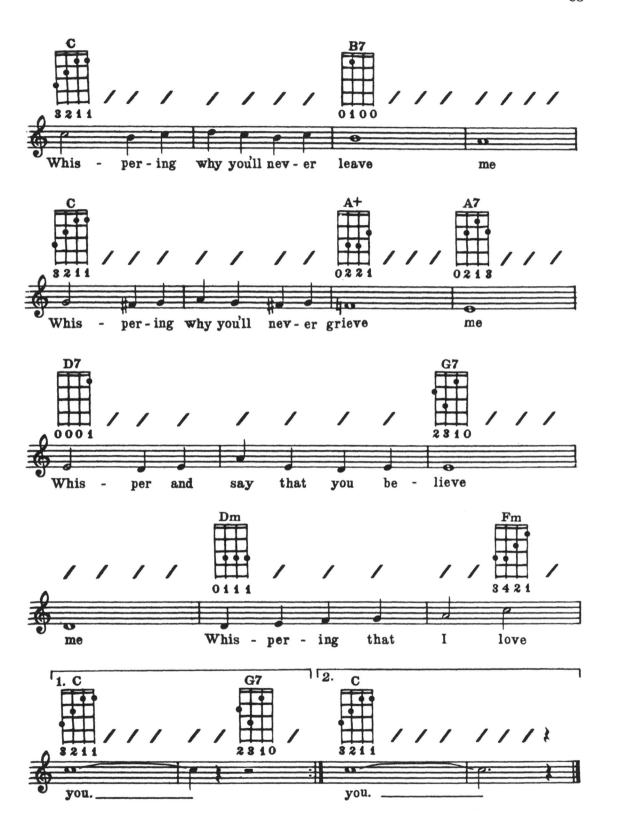

When I Grow Too Old To Dream

Lyric by
OSCAR HAMMERSTEIN II

Music by
SIGMUND ROMBERG

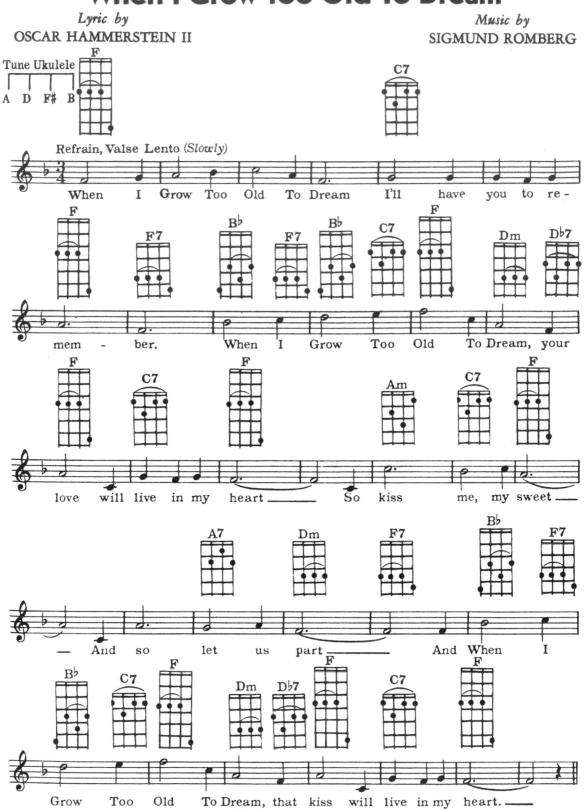